A Glitch in the System

Also by Adrienne Cosgrave and published by Ginninderra Press
I Have Secrets

Adrienne Cosgrave

A Glitch in the System

To Adam, Guy and Nat
always with love

A Glitch in the System
ISBN 978 1 76109 282 4
Copyright © text Adrienne Cosgrave 2022
Cover image: Karen Laårk Boshoff from Pexels

First published 2022 by
GINNINDERRA PRESS
PO Box 3461 Port Adelaide 5015
www.ginninderrapress.com.au

Contents

Inside	7
Inertia	8
Prey	9
Edge	10
Celebrity	12
Names	13
Best	14
Games	15
Am	16
Defiance	18
Beau	19
Mine	20
Complicit	21
White	22
Crush	24
Relief	25
Less	26
Conflict	27
Viral	28
Alone	30
Reverie	31
Reunion	32
Memory	34
RMC	36
Gone	37

Inside

There is the faint hum of traffic
from the bridge
and the morning sun is warm on the blind.

We have no place to see
and no one to be
but just us;
cosy and content as cats
in half-sleep.

The wind skips through the trees.

Somewhere a dog barks.

And I'm trailing my fingers across your skin,
so light it's barely a touch;
just a whisper of air between us.

You stir,
smile,
skooch close

and I'm thinking
that I could live
in this moment
always.

Inertia

Caught hard and fast
in a somebody sanctioned
kung fu grip.

Slap bang in the middle
of a year that never was.

Days shredded.
Months shelved.

Watching the clock.
Tick tock.

Outside is unyielding.

Rapunzel with a buzz cut
gazing out to sea.

See?

That's me.

Stevie Smith not waving.

Prey

In another time,
another place,
I might have been a contender.

Right height
right weight
long hair
clear face;

a perfect printout from your playbook.

Hidden fractures,
small distractions;

fodder for the foothills,
easy pickings for the eagle-eyed.

Like all those other girls
with names and people.

All those bright young girls
ended
in blunt brutality;
a shudder in the shadows.

All those pretty long ago girls
who did nothing wrong

save occupy
another time
another space.

Edge

Without you here,
I have lost my bearings
and the cosmetic seems redundant.

What does it matter?

I have no one to dress for,
no one to undress;
no one to kiss
with either passion or regret.

Days fall through my fingers
and evaporate;
cool and insubstantial.

I watch the ivy
snake and trail its way across the path;
the bamboo blustering through
from under the fence.

A thin winter sun teases my skin.

And I'm wondering how it might be
to just disappear.

To disown all tenses
and see my memory unwind.

Maybe a short sharp slice
and I could slip, so seamlessly,
into silence.

Ophelia without flowers.

Cleopatra collapsing.

My oblivion only you.

Celebrity

Somebody called you breathtaking
and within minutes
the whole world knew.

In your reluctant celebrity
your inscrutable manner
as an everyman
you are breathtaking.

In the battle for car park supremacy
and the seduction of supermarket shelves
you are breathtaking.

In the diurnal wait for school pickup
and the jibber jabber
of gossip and scandal
you are breathtaking.

In some secret heart
you are breathtaking.

How odd it must feel
for you to know
you can stem life's
oft time humdrum flow
and in faraway strangers
spark a glow

just by being breathtaking.

Names

you can tell me I'm winter
or needle-sharp rain
you can call me a banshee
who howls through your veins

you can string out my errors
to redeem your own pain
you can call out what's lacking
and haul up my shame

you can call me Miranda

you can call me Elaine

you can call me Medusa

but that's not my name

Best

On our best days
we are unstoppable,

inseparable,

bold as brass,
hot as blue blazes,
smooth as schmaltz;

the coolest cats with all the cream.

Thick as thieves
cruising the night,
we create our own code
and send the rest of the world to hell.

And as we grow older,
just over our shoulder,
we cast only one shadow
and a halo of light.

From the moment we met,
we were inevitable

and on our best days,
I think,
we could live forever.

Games

You take such offence
when I say you're intense
you call me aloof
but it's just my defence
you bring me conditions
and wait to collect
you pose cryptic questions
I cannot contest
you want for me freedom
but at your behest
and you lead me to feel
that I'm just like the rest
who spurned you or burned you
denied you success
then you badger with silence
until I confess

but

some learned behaviour
is hard to divest
it seeps through the subconscious
a con manifest
so the crap in your head
I can safely reject

I know what's in your heart

Am

I doodle hearts and flowers,
but my thoughts are murky,

sombre and ill-omened;
black crows watching over mourners
at a Victorian graveside.

I harbour odd confessions
and nurture small obsessions;
weeding and feeding
until I move on.

I don't move on.

I am plagued and hindered
by everything
and nothing
and my demons self-perpetuate
to reinforce my own myth.

I am broken
and mended
and broken again

and I replay my history
over and over.

I am bemused by the complexities
that run beneath my skin
and amused by the absurdity of existence.

I am a loser and a leper;
an unheralded success.
And I wonder if my dreams
could be a portal to the future.

But really, I am just matter decomposing,
a glitch in the system.

So, I light another cigarette
and ponder all creation,
simply filling in time
until my ultimate erasure.

Defiance

I approach you with some trepidation;
sure fear of more manipulation.
You're flipping through your dissertation,
a rigmarole of remonstration,
counting on my hesitation,
a space to fill with stipulations;
and waiting on my confirmation,
surrender to your complications.

But then, you know, my concentration
far outweighs your self-inflation;
I'm stronger than your affectation,
your sly attempts at orchestration.
I'm privy to your machinations,
the underlying implications.
So, where you seek capitulation,
I muster up determination.

I care not for expostulation,
subscription to your publication.
You offer me no revelation;
I'll spin my own interpretation.
I will not stoop to domination,
fall victim to your calculation.
I'm handing in my resignation
to launch a new investigation.

What happens next – my destination –
is not for your appropriation.

Beau

You were hopeful that night.

Spruced.

Ready to find fact in your fiction.

Looking back,
I can see how I might have broken your heart
a little;

chipped a small piece away
and let it fall;

debris,

discarded.

And in the arrogant oblivion of youth,
it never even occurred to me
that I had.

Mine

I watch.

I wait.

I follow.

Gathering gossip
like plump, ripe berries;

a sweetness to be savoured.

Calling on divine intervention.

Praying for a line of intersection.

To shimmer in the light of inception.

So I can breathe in the depth of your presence,

cradle your scars

and soothe the shiver in your soul.

I'd fuck all and give all for you;

if only you knew I were here,

watching

waiting

following.

Complicit

I should never have questioned your majesty,

your influence,

the logic you wear,
sharp
as a well-pressed suit.

You collect my thoughts,
twisting and weaving
into a cat's cradle of your own design.

You pick my bones clean
and smother my senses.

You scatter me sideways
and watch me roll.

Then you gather me up
with a hug
and a shrug
and a fresh demand;

knowing only the smirk of victory,
the insinuation of my defeat.

Yet still,
I question your majesty;

even as I enable it.

White

So this is how I live now.

With a rush of panic,
a wave of apathy,
a depletion of faith.

Tossing coins in a fountain,
a martyr to my own imaginings,
eyes cast to the heavens
like a saint on some long-ago holy card,
looking for a smile from Jesus,
a rapture that will never come.

There are mottos and mantras aplenty,
at hand, should I choose to recite,
but they hold no magic,
seem stale and worn,
a mere rattle of words
to be rolled like dice.

I remain earthbound,
fractured,
left in the lurch.

Still,
I picture you waiting,
on the other side,
in another life,
as a warm enveloping force.

And we can be Sunday morning,
so lazy and light;
a honeymoon couple for always,
in our own small corner of white.

Crush

I imagine us walking

side by side

a little apart

just shooting the breeze

our surrounds incidental

and a sweet stir of heat makes me blush

when I think what might happen

because I hope it would happen

do you think it could happen

should we touch?

Relief

Out on a limb.
Out on a cay.

The sun beats
without mercy
on a boatload of strangers
and the sand is prickled
with shell shards.

And I'm pushing hard
against the blue, blue sea,
lungs taut,
muscles bruised,
the reef running below me;
an eerie pulsing netherworld
of which I want no part.

But when I surface,
there you are.
Waiting.
So sure
against the curve of the horizon.

The foreign fringe falls away
and it could be just we two,
happily stranded on the edge of the world.

Less

no love
no life
no husband
no wife
no heart
no hope
no room
no scope
no fuel
no fire
no faith
no messiah
no rhythm
no dance
no point
no chance
no legs
no feet
no you
less me

Conflict

I am cornered.

Beset and besieged.

A field mouse caught
in a falcon's claws,

an impala too close
to a cheetah's jaws,

a soldier short
of winning the war,

an inch away
from risking it all;

and a chorus urges to make the call.

I feel cornered.

Embattled,
beleaguered,
beholden;

but not yet benign.

Viral

Political evangelists at 7 p.m.

Righteous,
indignant
and oh-so concerned.

Gathering grievances like trading cards
to be sorted and prized,
then swapped for some hashtagged indulgence
and a global crusade.

A Big Brother network
that never stops to blink/think.
Moments snapped out of context;
fodder for a faceless posse,
primed and poised for a lynching.

Nobodies watching
nobodies watching
nobodies become
somebodies
within a bubble of corrupted reality.

Ad slogans gone mantra.
Shifting genders.
Narcissists and princesses:
owed it all
and wanting it now.

Subtle manipulation.
Slow disintegration.

No grace.
No mystery.
No allure.

Just post.
Paste.
In your face.

Whaddup bitches?

Whatever it is,
there will be a swarm
all over it.

Gotta say,
I'm over it all.

Alone

The past is, indeed, a different country
and the further it recedes,
the more I want to live there.

But memory can be a sorcerer
        and a thief,
a braggart toying with truth

and perhaps mine is skewed
for want of you.

My solitude has become
a pair of red shoes,
a goose girl barrel lined with nails,
my ultimate undoing.

All true fairy tales require sacrifice;
are dark and brutal at the edges.

I know only
that once upon a time
held the promise of your touch,
the warmth of your presence,
the ineffable wanderings of your mind

and that now,
stark realities are scratching at my door
and I am so very tired,

lonely,

alone.

Reverie

I have a dream.

It can have no global impact,
will not better humanity,

but it is simple
and lucid
and mine.

Just only to wake
wherever you are.

To adore.

To be adored.

Reunion

An odd gathering, really.
A little vague and uneasy.

Familiar strangers.
Strange familiars.
Unspoken apologies
and tender regrets.

Small schoolyard clusters
that have reformed
through eerie habit.

Pilgrims at a shrine to memory.

And you're sporting an appropriate smile
for those you once secretly snubbed.

The one most likely to,
eyes darting,
seeking out favourites,
but without the flex or flourish of youth
and not yet willing to reveal
the conceits and errors
that brought you back.

Desperation?

Consolation?

Or confirmation
that once you were epic,
spinning sterling scenarios

for future selves;
secure in the seduction of your sell;
 the world would swoon and surrender.

But fate is fickle,
time heals nothing
and fortune favours precious few.

So what's the story
to your misplaced glory?

Did reality bite too hard?

Hold you hostage
on the names of your children?

Maybe ground you down
like a prison bitch,
leaving you broken,

anonymous

and wondering

how all that promise
could morph into something
so very ordinary.

Memory

I have no use for keepsakes,
or rosemary for remembrance.

What's to forget?

I saw your eyes flicker and dim.

I watched you disappear.

I am impaled on memory
and I fear I am bleeding out.

I knit.
I unravel.
I seek solace.

In the single strand of spider's silk
stretching from the shrubs to the veranda.

In the switch and squall of cold air
that rips the guts
from summer's flat, dry heat.

In the thirty seconds of sunshine
before grey clouds converge.

And I tell myself things could always be worse
        (which they could)

and to be thankful for small mercies
        (which I am)

but it is scant consolation
and no compensation
for a day

when Death crept through the house
so quietly
we didn't even know he was there.

RMC

You were
my most awesome adventure.

An architect, prince
and slayer of beasts.

You were Dylan and Lennon,
Zeppelin and Floyd;
my *Catch 22*
and my Neo.

Deft of hand,
fleet of mind
and true of heart,
with an absolute fuck you
fearless edge;

but you could never quite hush
those errant voices
that loitered like teens
inside your head.

Gone

I feel in part
that I've left you behind
we don't talk so much now
and our history's defined
and yet even so
after all of this time
it is visions of you
that devour my mind

www.ingramcontent.com/pod-product-compliance
Lightning Source LLC
Chambersburg PA
CBHW062207100526
44589CB00014B/1993